The Recovery of a
Contagious
Methodist
Movement

What people are saying about
The Recovery of a Contagious Methodist Movement

"This book is a passionate prophetic call to action and involvement in recapturing John Wesley's game plan for transforming a dying mainline institution into a vibrant and life-changing apostolic movement."
—Dr. Pat Day, Senior Pastor, First United
Methodist Church, Shreveport, Louisiana

"George Hunter has a fever and the only prescription is a Methodism revitalized as a missional movement of the Holy Spirit! From his vast knowledge of our church, as well as his extensive experience in global Christianity, Hunter makes a spirited case for Methodism on the move. Don't read this book if you don't want to catch the gospel contagion that George has got."
—Will Willimon, Bishop, Birmingham (AL) Area,
The United Methodist Church and prolific author

"George Hunter's *The Recovery of a Contagious Methodist Movement* challenges the assumptions of the *Call to Action*. From the vantage point of deep insight, Hunter argues that our current diagnosis and solutions betray an institutional bias, neglecting the best insights currently available. Those who care about Methodism as a movement for Christ and the advancement of the kingdom of God in this bruised and battered world will discover great insight for our shared mission."
—Bishop Mike Lowry, Resident Bishop of the Central
Texas Conference, The United Methodist Church

"This book will be valuable to the training of ministry leaders. It has helped me articulate what can be felt in an apostolic church. Chuck Hunter has provided a deeper understanding of the "why" behind the Methodist church's journey but more importantly has given a concise understanding of key principles and processes of the Wesleyan movement, which shape the movement of Christ's church and are in action around the world today."
—Craig W. Robertson, Founding Partner, Spiritual Leadership, Inc.

The Recovery of a
Contagious
Methodist
Movement

George G. Hunter III

Abingdon Press
Nashville

THE RECOVERY OF A CONTAGIOUS METHODIST MOVEMENT

This book is printed on acid-free paper.

Library of Congress Cataloging-in-Publication Data

Hunter, George G., 1938–
  The recovery of a contagious Methodist movement / George G. Hunter III.
    p. cm.
  Includes bibliographical references.
  ISBN 978-1-4267-4038-1 (pbk. : alk. paper)   1. Church renewal—United Methodist Church (U.S.)
2. United Methodist Church (U.S.)   3. Methodism.   I. Title.
  BX8382.2.H87 2011
  262'.076—dc23

2011031069

Scripture quotations are from the Common English Bible. Copyright © 2011 by the Common English Bible. All rights reserved. Used by permission. (www.CommonEnglishBible.com)

11 12 13 14 15 16 16 17 18 19 20—10 9 8 7 6 5 4 3 2 1

MANUFACTURED IN THE UNITED STATES OF AMERICA

To Leroy Howe

CONTENTS

FOREWORD

I entered the Candler School of Theology in the fall of 1960. I was assigned a roommate and a room in the dormitory for theologs. George "Chuck" Hunter entered seminary that same year. We met one afternoon jogging on the track at Emory. Chuck wasn't very fast so I slowed down to his pace. We had a great conversation and rapidly became good friends.

After the first quarter, my roommate and his roommate both dropped out of seminary. When I came back from the Christmas holidays, Chuck had moved into my room. We spent three years as roommates. Upon graduation we were both single, had no debt, had good grades, so we decided to go to Princeton Seminary for an additional graduate degree. I know Chuck Hunter well.

Finishing Princeton, he went to the Florida Conference and I went to the Alabama–West Florida Conference. We both became engaged in local church work. We didn't see each other often. Much to our surprise when we reconnected a few years later, we both had an intense interest in evangelism and church growth. We both began to pursue this study and practice. He was the teaching theologian. I tried to be the local church practitioner.

Chuck Hunter is one of the most articulate theologians in The United Methodist Church today. He has always sounded a clarion call for The United Methodist Church to remember our purpose for existence and to carry out the great commission. His many books on different aspects of evangelism have convicted, corrected, and convinced lay people and clergy of the priority of evangelism.

The Denman Lectures are a brief snapshot of the scope of Chuck Hunter's research, analysis, experience, and ability to articulate future trends. They are written for twenty-first-century evangelism. These lectures point to the depth of the theological issues involved and the practical application for local churches.

Chuck's passion is for the local church. His teaching, writing, and preaching all point to equipping pastors and laity for effective evangelism in the local church. Although he has not served a local church in many years, he has always stayed close to people serving in the local church in order to keep his thoughts and emphases grounded in areas that are applicable to the local church.

Chuck Hunter and I heard Harry Denman preach. Harry Denman was real and effective. Chuck has updated many of the basic theological and biblical concepts of Harry Denman so pastors and laypersons can be effective evangelists today. His lectures point to the very issues confronting The United Methodist Church today. He has the ability to analyze movements and directions within the sphere of evangelism. He also has the courage to point out fallacies in some of the proposals for evangelism. His writings are never from a negative critical perspective, but rather an invitation to make evangelism normative and effective in the local church.

While the lectures are a tribute to Harry Denman and George Hunter, their endearing effectiveness will be because they point to the One who gave us the great commission.

John Ed Mathison
www.johnedmathison.org

PREFACE

As I write this, I am pushing seventy-three. I am not especially nostalgic, but lately I have reflected on a lifetime of involvement in the service of Christianity's apostolic ministry. The seeking grace of God, and the ministry of a Methodist church in Miami, Florida, found me when I was a lost teenager who could not find the Way by myself. Within days of discovering new life, I knew I was called to some role in helping other people find their Way.

I prepared for years to make my contribution—including two theology degrees and a PhD in communication studies. More important, I was mentored by several giants in the field—especially Larry Lacour, Donald Soper, Bryan Green, and Donald McGavran, and occasionally by notables like Harry Denman, Stephen Neill, E. Stanley Jones, Kermit Long, Alan Walker, Ken Chafin, Bruce Larson, and my first dean Joe Quillian. I have been standing on at least a dozen sets of big shoulders for over thirty years!

I have spent a career in leadership, teaching, and scholarship in the related fields of Evangelization, Church Growth, and Missiology. I have published a dozen books in these fields. This book is my shortest, but I have packed it with more insight per page than in any other book. It goes to the printer with more hope than I have attached to any other book.

Earlier versions of the three chapters were presented as the Denman Lectures at the 2011 United Methodist Congress on Evangelism that convened in Myrtle Beach, South Carolina. The Denman Lectureship is a great tradition; it may be the largest attended lectureship in American

Protestant Christianity. I was aware that I lectured on the fortieth anniversary of Albert Outler's celebrated series, "Evangelism in the Wesleyan Spirit." This project stands on his shoulders.

I have engaged in some revisions for printing, but have retained much of the language of an orally delivered lectureship. Friends like Carol Childress, Jim Heidinger, Ken Kinghorn, Steve Martyn, and Lyle Schaller gave invaluable feedback from their reading of an early draft. Many people at the Congress asked questions and gave feedback that stimulated revisions. I need to thank other people collectively, including colleagues at the Methodist Board of Evangelism, the Perkins School of Theology at SMU, the United Methodist Board of Discipleship, and Asbury Seminary's E. Stanley Jones School of World Mission and Evangelism.

Several ideas pervade this book: Methodism was once a great contagious movement in North America. Our current mess in United Methodism, and in mainline Christianity generally, is the consequence of many choices over time. The way forward will involve more informed choices in the service of a renewed apostolic vision. Although Methodism has a remarkable and storied history, it is possible for its future to be greater; a greater future is not assured, nor even probable, but it is clearly possible.

I hope that this small book is destined to help inform the choices that can restore, for our time, a version of Methodism that becomes a contagious movement once again. If, however, you are certain that The United Methodist Church and the other mainline denominations are currently on the right track, this book is not (yet) for you. Save your money!

Chapter One

CHRISTIANITY ACCORDING TO THE WESLEYS

The Denman Lectureship is presented periodically in honor of Harry Denman, who headed the Methodist Church's Board of Evangelism from 1939 to 1965. Mr. Denman was a layman, a giant in Methodism, and a world legend. Early in his career, he was the "church manager" of First Methodist Church in Birmingham, Alabama, from 1919 to 1939. When Arthur Moore became the senior pastor in 1926, Moore and Denman became an awesome leadership team. In a ten-year period, the church averaged receiving more than ten new Christians a week.

In the late 1930s, the Methodist Episcopal Church, the Methodist Episcopal Church, South, and the Methodist Protestant Church were finalizing the merger that became The Methodist Church. One urban legend reports that the Southern bishops wanted a Board of Evangelism and the Northern bishops did not. The Northern bishops finally agreed, but only if the new denomination named a layman as its general secretary. The Southern bishops agreed, and smiled; they'd had Harry Denman in mind all along!

"Old Harry" was a lifelong bachelor. He lived and modeled the simple Christian life; he usually owned just one suit. He led the Board of Evangelism for twenty-six years. Denman and his colleagues developed programs of evangelism that were strategically appropriate for the time. For instance, hundreds of thousands of people were reached by "Two by Two" evangelism, in which a Methodist team of two people visited everyone in a neighborhood, door to door. In time, American society changed; resistance to door-to-door visitors, high-rise apartments, gated communities, and other changes phased out the Two by Two era. But Denman and his colleagues did not only make their contribution through programs, manuals, and flip charts. Mainly, they found ways to remind American Methodism of its main business in the tradition of John Wesley. In the years following Denman's retirement, the next denominational merger reduced his board to one of eight program sections within a new conglomerate board. It may not be entirely coincidental that we have experienced continuous net membership decline ever since.

The decade of the 1940s was the golden era of afternoon radio for kids. My buddies and I listened to programs like Tom Mix, Batman, the Green Hornet, the Lone Ranger, and Jack Armstrong the All American Boy. But our favorite was Superman. We all knew that the story was fiction, because Clark Kent spent most of his time as "a mild mannered reporter." But we were hooked because we knew that, in every episode, sooner or later, some great evil would threaten the city of Metropolis. In the nick of time, Clark Kent would enter a telephone booth and strip off his outer clothing. Then, with the "S" showing and the cape flowing, he was transformed into "The Man of Steel." Suddenly, the announcer explained, our super hero became "faster than a speeding bullet, more powerful than a locomotive, and able to leap tall buildings in a single bound!" Every day, without fail, Superman rescued the city from destruction just a minute or two before the half-hour program was scheduled to end. We were enthralled.

The 1940s were also the golden era of the ten-cent comic book for kids; my favorite was Captain Marvel. At one level, Captain Marvel seemed like a Superman clone. For example, his alter ego, Billy Batson, was a radio news reporter and, when he was in the super hero role, he also wore tights and a cape. Below the similarities, however, a distinctive narrative carried each issue of the Captain Marvel comic book.

A three-thousand-year-old Egyptian wizard, Shazam, had fought evil for three millennia. As he now neared the end of his life, he deputized Billy Batson to continue his work. The wizard entrusted to Billy Batson the insight and the key to become a super hero whenever it was necessary. The key was the wizard's name—*Shazam*—which was an acronym of the first letters in the names of six heroes of antiquity: Solomon, Hercules, Atlas, Zeus, Achilles, and Mercury. From Solomon, Billy Batson would receive wisdom, from Hercules he received strength, from Atlas—stamina, from Zeus—power, from Achilles—courage, and from Mercury he received speed.

The wizard coached Billy Batson to focus on the acronym, SHAZAM, and to use it to get in conscious touch with all that the wizard had taught him about these six legendary figures. Then, when Billy uttered the word SHAZAM, their wisdom, strength, stamina, power, courage, and speed would emerge from the past, fill him, and empower him for superhuman achievement. SHAZAM!

As kids of ten or eleven, we never once believed in what we knew was fiction, but, like in all theater, we suspended our disbelief so the story could live for a while in our imaginations. Nevertheless, I learned something from the Captain Marvel comics that escaped many people of my generation, and of this generation. In many subtle ways, the past is still much with us. William Faulkner contended, "The past is never dead; it's not even past." Whether or not his statement exaggerates, the past is at least more relevant and available than we usually imagine. And by rooting ourselves in the past, we may discover sources of wisdom, virtue, insight, perspective, vision, and power, some of which are not usually as available in the present.

TOWARD REDISCOVERING WESLEY AND EARLY METHODISM

Methodists also have a six-letter word to recall. When people of the Methodist way get in touch with that word and all that we know in connection with it, we gain a perspective and strength that fill us from the past and empower us for extraordinary achievement. That six-letter word is W-E-S-L-E-Y.

I am not suggesting, as some have, that John Wesley is our ultimate authority. Wesley, after all, never claimed or aspired to produce an original form of Christianity. His magnificent obsession was simply to recover the gospel, the theology, the vision, the mission, and the contagion of early Apostolic Christianity. His tombstone, in London, reminds us that he simply wanted "to enlighten these nations, and to revive, enforce, and defend the pure apostolic doctrines and practices of the primitive Church." John Wesley can still teach us more about how to go about that than anyone who has come along since.

Furthermore, I am not suggesting that we should do everything exactly as the eighteenth-century Methodists did, any more than they did everything exactly as the New Testament churches did. They knew that contexts and conditions change so much over time that simply restoring yesterday is seldom the best way forward. At the basic level of principles, however, and strategic insights that can be adapted to any context, Wesley has much to teach us. He is the only apostolic genius in Methodism's relatively brief history. If we stand on his shoulders, we will see the way forward in our time.

Once upon a time, in John Wesley's lifetime and for another century or more, Methodism in Great Britain and in North America was a contagious Christian movement. In Wesley's lifetime, early British Methodism grew from scratch in 1739 to reach 140,000 converts by his death in 1791; British Methodism grew in the succeeding generations, while spreading to many other countries.

Meanwhile, laymen brought Methodism to the colonies. When their letter asked Wesley for help in 1784, he commissioned twenty-six-year-old Francis Asbury for America. Asbury knew Wesley's mind, was immersed in Wesley's writings, and when he had to make a strategic decision, he seems to have asked, "What would Mr. Wesley advise?" When Asbury arrived in 1784, there were 1200 Methodists in America; by his death in 1816, there were 214,000 American Methodists. This apostolic momentum continued for a very long time; in the quarter century from 1880 to 1905, American Methodism averaged planting over seven hundred new churches per year. As late as the 1920s, the world mission of American Methodism was deploying over twenty-five hundred foreign missionaries.

These Methodist achievements, on both sides of the Atlantic, contrasted remarkably with the more institutionalized expressions of Christianity. Before Wesley's time, the Church of England made parish churches available to most of England's people, but the national church lacked anything like a missionary identity or priority. The people perceived the church to offer little more than baptisms, weddings, and funerals, so most of the people only came to church to be "hatched, matched, and dispatched." The Anglican Church and British culture casually assumed that, by definition, England was a "Christian" country, so every baptized and confirmed member of an Anglican parish was, by definition, a "Christian."

This became, essentially, the policy of every national or culturally privileged church in Europe—Western Europe and Eastern Europe. Furthermore, establishment Christianity everywhere seemed to assume that the way they did church was exactly what Jesus and the apostles had in mind. John Wesley, however, perceived that the policy was fallacious. Soren Kierkegaard was to express Wesley's reservations even more memorably: "When everybody is a Christian, nobody is a Christian." While Kierkegaard's point is almost self-evident, it bears restating. When everybody in a so-called Christian culture is assumed to be a Christian, this assumption immunizes people against the possibility of becoming actual followers of Jesus Christ. Kierkegaard observed that his native Denmark featured "a full inventory" of priests, bishops, churches, organs, and so on but, he grieved, "the Christianity of the New Testament . . . does not exist."

Does enough New Testament Christianity exist in any institutional form of Christianity, including The United Methodist Church, to change the world, or even to substantially change half of the people who already subscribe to it? Although Methodism started out as a missional alternative to establishment Christianity and sustained its movemental momentum longer than might have been predicted, it has now become the establishment Christianity that it once critiqued.

Can a once great movement, which over time devolved into a more sterile institutional form, become a contagious movement once again? If so, what would that look like? Consider these four themes, beginning with the most obvious.

WESLEYAN THEOLOGY

Movemental Methodism would substantially share John Wesley's theological perspective. Classical Methodism was shaped and driven by a cluster of theological convictions.

The most obvious of these is the supreme importance of the Scriptures. Although Wesley was one of the most widely read public men of his century, he regarded himself as "a man of one book." A Methodist's mind and heart are rooted in the biblical revelation. Wesley was not into "biblioatry," but he experienced the Bible as having normative authority—without ever claiming any theory of the Scriptures that "proved" its authority. He also experienced the Scripture's sacramental power to catalyze faith and deepen faith; as the Scriptures' writers were inspired, so the Holy Spirit inspires those who study the Scriptures.

Wesley's view of the authority of Scripture has been somewhat obscured since the early 1970s by the misuse of what Albert Outler famously called the Wesleyan Quadrilateral. Outler observed that Scripture, tradition, reason, and experience are the general sources for theological reflection in the Methodist tradition. (Outler was simply acknowledging the addition of experience to the Anglican Trilateral.) In time, however, some United Methodist leaders decided that the four sources were equal, and some leaders even made experience their priority source—with Scripture now subordinated to their experience-based reasoning. This move opened the door to two problems. One problem is the widespread assumption that no one theological perspective could possibly be normative, because all theological perspectives are created equal. The other problem is the ensuing theological anarchy that now confuses anyone in the wider world who still listens to United Methodism.

Wesley's theological roots were biblical, though his sources for theological reflection were extensive. He read the early church fathers, Eastern and Western, and he affirmed the early creeds. Even though he regarded himself as an evangelical Anglican, he studied other traditions—including Roman Catholic, Eastern Orthodox, Lutheran, and Reformed. His knowledge of other Christian traditions helped him clarify and refine his own theological vision.

What are the enduring, towering, and indispensable themes of John Wesley's Christian theology? Albert Outler, preaching at Baltimore's Lovely Lane Church on the Sunday during the 1984 General Conference, identified three such themes: original sin, grace, and sanctification. In the best one minute of theological analysis I have ever heard, Outler interpreted the more recent history of American Methodism from those three themes. American Methodism, he said, produced two great movements—the nineteenth-century Holiness movement and twentieth century Liberalism. By 1984, he observed that both movements were "spent forces." The Holiness movement was spent because it remembered the first and third of Wesley's themes but forgot the second. Liberalism was spent because it remembered the second theme, but forget the first and third.

It is hard to imagine any way that American Methodism will ever recover its mojo without recovering John Wesley's theological vision. It's not that we haven't tried other ways. Boston Personalism, as one example, once represented a serious move to substantially replace Wesley's theological perspective with another. Personalism was a fairly impressive philosophical and theological achievement. Many churches that spoke from Personalism's script engaged a generation's questions, and the churches experienced some vitality and growth. But that school of thought had a shelflife of one generation, and the later parade of new theologies have often experienced little more than their fifteen minutes of fame.

At one point in its history, following the 1968 merger of The Methodist Church and The Evangelical United Brethren Church that became The United Methodist Church, Methodism was substantially, and quietly, steered toward a generic mainline destination. What I am about to report was never prominent in the public discussions before, or after, the merger. In those years, I was on the staff of the Board of Evangelism, and then on the Perkins faculty, and then on the staff of the Board of Discipleship. In those years, some senior denominational executives were informing staff people that what the merger was really about was becoming a "New Church." These leaders were good people who meant well; like leader-groups in most generations, they convinced themselves that they knew best. So becoming a New Church would involve one major shift: our church would become much less Methodist and much more mainline—like the Presbyterians, Lutherans, Episcopalians, and so on.

We had already drifted in that direction; now we were being navigated in that direction. Ironically, much of Methodism's theological academy was becoming *more* Methodist; scholars like Albert Outler, William R. Cannon, and Frank Baker produced the greatest generation of Wesleyan scholarship. But a constellation of denominational executives agreed that they knew better than the early Methodists and their own scholars. The accelerated shift from a Methodist to a mainline identity did not just happen. We were pushed.

Indeed, in those years, the 1970s and 1980s, we managed to become more mainline than our partners. Today, Lutherans are more consciously and recognizably Lutheran, Presbyterians—Presbyterian, and Episcopalians—Anglican, than United Methodists are consciously and recognizably Methodist. We gave up much more than our partners did in the hope that they would welcome us into the mainline club of denominations.

But how has the decision to become less Methodist and more mainline worked out for us? Two outcomes have become obvious.

First, most of the other major mainline churches migrated from national churches in Europe; for them, it made some sense to perpetuate a form of European Christianity in this land. Methodists, however, did not come from a European national church. We came from an apostolic movement within the Church of England; and we only became a "church" after the Church of England, following Wesley's death, encouraged our exodus. We gave up much more than the others to be welcomed into the mainline.

Second, in the wake of the decision to become much less Methodist and much more mainline, we have experienced over forty years of membership decline. Scott Kisker's prophetic book, *Mainline or Methodist*, observes, "When we became mainline, we stopped actually being Methodists in all but name." He observes how the shift to the mainline has sucked much of the identity, vitality, and reproductive power out of our once-great movement. Kisker adds, "For us in so-called mainline Methodism, our 'mainline' identity is killing us and we must surgically remove it if we are ever to regain our health."

An additional consequence of the denomination's shift to the mainline now haunts many of our churches. Most of the people who are still in our churches are afflicted with amnesia. They cannot recall what we believe—if, indeed, most of them ever knew. Moreover, with the possible exception of our polity, they have no idea who we are as Methodists. Another consequence is that we cannot observe, anywhere, a long line of people eager to join a church that does not know what it believes, or who it is, or so easily changes its mind.

I sympathize with the growing chorus of people who believe that if United Methodism became more theologically Wesleyan again, we would salvage our sinking ship. If only it were that simple. We all wish, of course, that one single intervention or solution could reform and renew churches. The supreme issue, however, is not only whether we can recover the theology of the Wesleys. Franz Hildebrandt had it right when he once challenged us to recover "Christianity according to the Wesleys."

The distinction between *theology* and *Christianity* is important because Christianity is more than theology. One reason United Methodism is stuck, stagnant, and declining is because we assume that American mainline Christianity gets everything else right except, perhaps, some of the theology. The problem is that the prevailing mainline paradigm for doing church is essentially an import from the European established-church tradition, which has an impressive pedigree and its own integrity, but is alien to classical Methodism. To be more specific, many United Methodist leaders who think of themselves as Wesleyan, are Wesleyan in theology only. When it comes to doing church, they assume that Wesley got it wrong, Europe's establishment churches got it right, and the American mainline churches have it right today.

I am proposing, however, that our recovery of Methodist Christianity and our move from institutional to movemental Christianity would involve the recovery of at least three bold directions in ministry, in addition to Wesley's theological vision.

LAY MINISTRIES

The early Methodism that spread across England, America, and elsewhere was essentially a lay movement. In Methodist Societies, most of the ministry that mattered was entrusted to laity. Indeed, most of the preachers were lay preachers; laity took on virtually all of a society's ministries and leadership. Several lay stewards governed each Methodist society. Early Methodism involved everyone, believers and seekers, in small groups called classes; the classes were lay led. Methodists who were really serious met in small groups called bands; the bands were lay led. The stewards, class leaders, band leaders, and other laypeople did most of the shepherding of local Methodists, everywhere.

Methodist laity also ministered far beyond the ranks of card-carrying Methodists. They reached out to the families and friends of Methodists. In the wider community, they visited from house to house. They visited prisoners and the families of prisoners. They visited people in hospitals and, during epidemics, Methodists were known to be the only people who cared enough and dared enough to visit the hospitals. Wherever they engaged in ministry, they also engaged in the ministry of evangelical conversation. They often prayed with people and they invited people to their class meeting or Methodist Society to explore the possibility of a new life.

Eighteenth-century Methodists were an entrepreneurial laity; lay people invented many ministries to serve people in their community. In some communities, lay Methodists gathered children to give them the only organized education they might ever experience. Lay people started most of the new classes and societies. Lay people brought Methodist

Christianity across the Atlantic. And when they wrote to Wesley, "Send some preachers to help us," they did not ask Wesley, "Send some preachers to do all the ministry for us!" That is, however, pretty much what most United Methodist churches ask their bishop to do today. In the last two centuries, we have experienced no greater shift than in our assumption about who does most of the ministry.

What caused this remarkable shift? How did Methodism morph from the most lay-centered Christian tradition to one of the most clergy-centered? One book is substantially responsible; it is the most influential book that most pastors today have never read. But our predecessors read it, and it has silently shaped theological education ever since. I am referring to *The Reformed Pastor*, by Richard Baxter, published in 1656. From several perspectives, it is such a wonderful book that its endurance is understandable; it is filled with the Scriptures, and the writer's devotion shines through every page. For two centuries, the book dominated in the education of Protestant clergy.

John Wesley knew Baxter's *The Reformed Pastor*, but he damned it with faint praise, and he mainly ignored it. Why? The book assumes, throughout, that virtually all of the ministry that matters is assigned to the ordained pastor. The book dramatizes how incomplete the Protestant Reformation of Luther and Calvin was. The job description of the Protestant pastor was essentially the same as for the medieval Roman Catholic priest. The priest's job was to care for the parish, hear confessions, and put the body and blood of Christ on people's tongues. Baxter defined the Protestant pastor's job as caring for the parish, doing pastoral counseling, and putting the Word of Christ in people's ears. It is a version of the same paradigm! Ministry is all about what the clergy do.

You would never know from Baxter's classic text that the people of God are the salt of the earth and the light of the world, or that the Holy Spirit "gifts" all of the members of the body of Christ for a range of ministries, or even that Luther's Reformation had once aspired to "the priesthood of all believers." Although, like the leaders of many Christian traditions, Baxter believed that his version of the Reformation had recovered New Testament Christianity, he was oblivious to the elementary fact that early Christianity was a lay movement. No one in the early Christian movement was ordained, in the sense that any tradition now means it, until the early third century. As a lay movement, early Christianity exploded across the Judean hills and, in time, won a majority of the urban citizens of an empire by persuasion alone.

John Wesley understood this clearly, and that is one reason why early Methodism was a lay movement without apology. Bruce Larson observed that across the earth today, wherever most of the ministry that matters is assigned to pastors and other religious professionals, the church is stagnant or declining; and wherever most of the ministry that matters is entrusted to the laity, the church is growing, even in astonishingly difficult circumstances—as in China.

So a rhetorical question seems necessary: Does American Methodism stand a fair chance of experiencing renaissance without recovering the ministry and mission of the laity?

SMALL GROUPS

In 1984, I gave a lecture series as one of several events in which Protestant Christians in South Korea were celebrating their centennial. The executive for the whole centennial was a Methodist minister and statesman, Dr. Byounghoon Kang. One Sunday I preached in his Namsan Methodist Church—which was planted in the early 1950s to reach and serve refugees from the tyranny in North Korea. I was moved to see the people, after thirty years, fervently praying for North Korea and their loved ones there. At lunch, Dr. Kang remarked that he did a D. Min. at Emory University, and he had preached in the USA on several occasions.

I asked him what he thought about Methodism in America. He replied, "From what I could tell, Methodism does not really exist in America." When he noticed my puzzled expression, he explained, "Your 'Methodist' churches do not have class meetings. Your people do not minister to each other through class meetings. In my church, and in most of our churches," he reported, "all of our people meet in class meetings. Our members' involvement in class meetings is even more important than their involvement in Sunday worship. Can there be real Methodism without class meetings?"

The next week, I interviewed eight other Korean Methodist pastors on this point. They all reported that virtually all of their members, and many seekers, meet regularly in class meetings. One pastor quoted John Wesley as saying that the class meeting is "the sinew (the connective tissue) of Methodism." I wrote that down and, later, I looked it up. Yep, that was Wesley's view all right!

Another pastor reflected, "If our people were not shepherding each other in their class meetings, the pastors would have to shepherd every-one. But we do not have enough pastors to do that. Many sheep would run wild, and many others would leave the flock." Then someone reminded me, that is how Pastor Cho and his people built Yoido Central Full Gospel Church into the world's largest church. Cho learned from the Methodist class meeting system, and their forty thousand home cell groups reached and nurtured most of the church's several hundred thousand members.

I suppose that every American church leader in our time has heard about small groups, and most leaders would regard them as desirable, but when I have asked, "What happens in your small groups?" American church leaders report a range of agendas or activities in small groups. They refer most often to Bible study groups, prayer groups, support groups, therapy groups, recovery groups, interest groups, and self-help groups. Church leaders usually assume that whatever their people do in small groups today is what early Methodists did in the class meetings. Let's examine that assumption.

If eighteenth century Methodist leaders could visit and advise us, they would rejoice when they saw people engaged and helped in Bible study groups, self-help groups, and so on. But they would report that their core agenda in class meetings was different. The Methodist class meeting typically followed three objectives: (1) The people who joined a class meeting were people who wanted to live a new life, as reflected in the three commitments to do good, to avoid evil, and to access the means of grace. (2) The people engaged in ministry with each other, in part to help each other live a Christian life. (3) The class meetings invited and welcomed pre-Christian people who also wanted to live a new life; with them, the members engaged in ministry and witness. The early Methodists believed that, in the class meetings, they had restored the koinionia of early Christianity's house churches.

Much more can be said for the complete restoration of something like the class meeting approach to small group life. My recent book, *The Apostolic Congregation*, attempts a cogent case for small group life:

Other important things happen in small group life, and not usually outside it. For instance, in small groups people discern each other's gifts for ministry. In small groups, people gain experience in lay ministry, and are more likely to minister to people outside the group, and outside the church. In small groups with an "empty chair" that they fill with a seeker every six months, small groups reach people; in many churches, the groups are the initial port of entry for far more seekers than a worship service. In small groups with a seeker or two in their fellowship, Christians gain experience in the ministry of Christian witness, and are more likely to engage in the ministry of witness outside the group, and outside the church. Leaders surface in small groups; leaders are developed in small groups. The whole church grows as it proliferates small groups. All of this (and more) is why more and more churches are becoming churches of small groups. This is why Bruce Larson used to say, "It is just as important to be involved in a small group as it is to believe that Jesus Christ died for your sins!"

MISSIONAL CHRISTIANITY

In contrast to the policy of the establishment Christianity that regarded every baptized member of the parish as a Christian, early Methodism was an extravagant expression of missional Christianity. What the Anglicans saw as a parish full of Christians, the Methodists saw as a mission field—filled with many people who had not understood the gospel, had not yet experienced justification, were not yet Christ-followers who lived by the will of God. Wesley perceived that a very great many people across England were "brutishly ignorant of the Christian faith. They give us no reason to believe that the faith that is not in their heads is in their hearts." Most of them, he observed, were not atheists; they were Deists. He regarded Deism as "a plague spread far and wide."

John Wesley redefined Christianity's main business. He taught his leaders, "You have nothing to do but save souls." He carefully explained what he meant:

> By salvation I mean, not barely, according to the vulgar notion, deliverance from hell, or going to heaven; but a present deliverance from sin, a restoration of the soul to its primitive health, its original purity; a recovery of the divine nature; the renewal of our souls after the image of God, in righteousness and true holiness, in justice, mercy and truth.

John Wesley, preaching from the Acts of the Apostles, defined "Scriptural Christianity, as beginning to exist in individuals; as spreading from one to another; as covering the earth." He believed that the ministry of evangelism to pre-Christian people, rightly understood, is the normal work of the whole church, all of the time, unless it has ceased being the church of Jesus Christ. Early Methodists understood that they were an ecclesia—the called out people of God; and they were also an *apostolate*— the sent out people of God.

What is especially distinctive in John Wesley's understanding of apostolic ministry is his understanding of how we help people become new Christians. Albert Outler called it Wesley's "Ordo Salutis." The Order of Salvation was not a theory only; it was also the practical model that informed Methodist outreach. They observed a process, involving four steps, in the typical conversion experience:

1. People are first *awakened* to the fact of their lostness, their sins, their need for the grace of God and their need for a new life.
2. Awakened people were then *enrolled* in a class (and, in three months—if they continued the quest—they were enrolled in a Methodist society). Their ongoing experiences with the class and

society will keep them awakened and prepare them for justification and second birth.

3. You teach awakened and enrolled people to expect to experience their *justification*. You help people expect that they will experience, at a time and manner of God's choosing, God's forgiveness and acceptance and the gifts of faith and new life.

4. You then teach justified people to expect to experience their *sanctification* in this life. They now expect that God will complete the work begun in their justification; the Spirit will free their hearts from sin's power, restore them to the people they were born to be, and free them to live their life in love by the will of God.

Wesley's preachers had an apostolic function, and public preaching was certainly an indispensable form for communicating the gospel. However, the salient purpose in much of the preaching, especially field preaching, was more to awaken people and begin the process, rather than to convert people on the spot—though, if that happened, it was welcomed!

But the Methodist preachers were only "playing coaches" for the Methodist laity who initially engaged at least 95 percent of the seekers who became Christians. And the laity mainly engaged pre-Christian people through outreach ministry, and especially the ministry of conversation. With Wesley's legendary status as a preacher, we may not remember that Wesley was at least as well known in his time as a conversationalist. Alexander Pope wrote, "I hate to meet up with John Wesley. The dog enchants you with his conversation, and breaks it off to go talk to an old woman." Wesley carried on an extensive ministry of conversation, including the ministry of letter writing. In his journal, he reflected, "After all our preaching, many of our people are almost as ignorant as if they had never heard the gospel. . . . I have found by experience, that one of these has learned more from one hour's close discourse, than from ten years' public preaching."

Methodism spread as a movement mainly through the credibility, ministry, and witness of the laity. Nineteenth-century Holiness evangelists observed, "Shepherds don't make new sheep, sheep make new sheep!" Evangelism especially happened through the class meetings. The autobiographical accounts of many eighteenth-century converts report that often, in their solitude in the hours following a class meeting, the Holy Spirit visited them and conferred the gift of faith.

In recent years, a new interest in *Missional Christianity* has surfaced; it is a buzzword in some circles. Everyone acknowledges that it involves evangelizing pre-Christian people, but some of the missional church literature says little about how. So let me conclude by summarizing three of the most important discoveries in the last generation in the study of effective Christian evangelism.

(1) For a very long time, Protestant Christianity has usually assumed a one-time model of evangelism. You preach or teach the gospel to someone, one time, and then you invite, and expect, a verdict for or against Christ, on the spot. Research has discovered, however, that conversion to Christian faith seldom takes place in the time span of one sermon, lesson, or conversation. There is virtually no *instant* evangelism. Increasingly, Christian conversion is understood as a process that typically moves through a chain of experiences over time—typically two or three seasons. Many church leaders regard the idea of *process* evangelism as a revolutionary new insight.

(2) The Protestant evangelical tradition has generally assumed a certain sequence in evangelism: You teach the gospel to people, then you invite them to accept it and, if they do, you then welcome them into the Christian fellowship. Three steps: proclamation, then invitation, then assimilation; almost everyone once assumed those steps, in that order. Research has demonstrated, however, that more and more people—especially postmodern people—have to *belong* before they *believe*. This model proposes a very different three-step sequence:

(a) You engage lost people on their turf; you begin conversation, and you invite them to your group or church.

(b) You welcome seekers into the fellowship, and they become involved in the life of the group and the church.

(c) In time, when they discover that they now believe, the church invites them to commit to what they now believe.

Many church leaders, also, have experienced this model as a revolutionary new insight.

(3) Donald McGavran's Church Growth movement has focused, for a generation, on the ground-breaking strategic principle that if the churches, in evangelism and mission, focused primarily on the most receptive people and populations, then the gospel would spread much more. In every season, receptive people—in whom the Spirit is moving, are the "harvest" that "the Lord of the harvest" is calling his church to gather. That one new principle has magnified the growth of many churches and missions, worldwide.

These three insights are not new insights. They are, essentially, old insights whose time has come once again.

For example, two and a half centuries before "belonging before believing" surfaced as a new idea, early Methodism was welcoming awakened seekers into the fellowship of class meetings, and into the life of Methodist societies, before they had believed or experienced anything. As Lord Soper used to say, early Methodists knew that the faith is "more caught than taught."

Furthermore, early Methodist leaders were at least as clear as any of us today that conversion is a process that involves a chain of experiences over time, and that Christians are called to understand, support, and nourish that process that leads to faith.

Moreover, two centuries before McGavran, John Wesley was teaching his people to find and reach lost people who are "ripe for the gospel." He coached Methodists to especially reach out to people who were already seeking truth and new life, and where there was already "fruit." "Go to those who want you; and go most to those who want you most."

These insights can be summarized in a game plan that any church can move with, and grow with:

1. Initiate conversation and ministry with pre-Christian people in the community.
2. Invest the most time with the people who are the most receptive.
3. Invite them into the life of Christian community.
4. Support their quest until they discover, in God's good time, the gift of faith.

These insights, and many others, can demonstrate that Christianity according to the Wesleys, with appropriate adaptations, can position American Methodism for a magnificent future. Who'd have thought it? Vision, strategy, and power from the past.

SHAZAM!

Chapter Two

WHAT CONTAGIOUS CHRISTIAN MOVEMENTS LOOK LIKE

In this book, we are reflecting around one question: How can Methodism, which was once a great apostolic movement, but is now a more stagnant institutional form of Christianity, become a contagious movement once again? The first chapter focused on the Wesleyan part of the question; this chapter focuses on the themes of *movement* and *contagion*.

I first proposed that we shift, big time, toward a version of "Christianity according to the Wesleys" that would fit our time and context, and that such a shift would involve both a substantial recovery of John Wesley's theological vision and a recovery of the contours of early Methodism's alternative approach to doing church: lay ministries, small groups, and apostolic ministry—locally and globally. Supremely, early Methodism was driven by the conviction that it is not a Christian movement's main business to protect the gospel from the pagans and barbarians; the gospel is entrusted to us for the sake of the pagans and barbarians. Furthermore, Methodists believed that it is not a local church's main business to nurture the members, important as that is; the church's main business is to make the new life of faith a live option for all the people who do not even know what we are talking about.

We are in the fifth decade of The United Methodist Church's year-by-year decline in membership strength. Although several successive General Conferences managed to ignore the elephant in the room, leaders are now asking how the denomination could become more viable again. An official committee of twenty denominational leaders has released a *Call to Action*; the *Call* focuses on some possible interventions that, if implemented, might make some difference.

The committee, however, seems to have asked a different question than the one now before us. The committee would probably acknowledge that Methodism was once more movemental but is now more institutional. The document, however, seems to share the entrenched assumption that Wesley and Kierkegaard once challenged: the assumption that institutional Christianity, whether in the European national church form or the American mainline form, is "normal" Christianity. So the committee seemed to ask *how can we re-introduce more vitality into the local churches of Institutional Methodism?*

The main problem with the committee's *Call* is that, if it succeeds, the denomination might only reduce the hemorrhaging, membership and attendance and finances might stabilize, and the denomination's executives might feel less heat. Let's pause a moment on the heat issue; something may be missing. Sam Rayburn, long time Speaker of the House of Representatives, used to say, "When I feel the heat, I see the light!"

The thinking behind such proposals as the *Call to Action* may need to be informed by additional light. If the *Call*, in its present form, is implemented at every level, the most optimistic possible outcome would still leave a shell of Methodism with some of the brain, more of the heart, and most of the vertebrate removed. We still would not represent a version of the faith that could change the world. How do we know that? It does not substantially change a majority of the people who already subscribe to it.

Let me compare institutional Christianity and movemental Christianity: Christianity in the tradition of the apostles penetrates communities as salt and light, it finds and engages lost populations on their turf, and it cares enough and dares enough to enter and reclaim "enemy territory." C. T. Studd, the British cricket star and mission leader, observed: "Most Christians remain within the sound of church and chapel bell, but I would rather run a rescue shop within a yard of hell." The *Call to Action* omits even an echo or a whisper of that kind of Christianity.

Furthermore, the *Call to Action* largely ignores what a more apostolic Methodism used to be, and achieve, in this land. We have already rehearsed early American Methodism's achievement. The story continued until fairly recent times. From 1880 to 1905, for instance, Methodism averaged planting over seven hundred new churches per year; these days, the last I checked, we plant about seventy a year. In the 1920s, we supported and deployed over 2,500 foreign missionaries; today, less than 400. As late as the 1950s, our churches received over 400,000 new Christians a year by profession of faith; today, less than 200,000.

Contrary to what most of us in United Methodism assume we know, our net membership decline has not been primarily due to losing more people than we used to, but rather to reaching fewer people than we used to. But more recently, that has changed some. Due to the graying of the denomination, we now lose more people each year to death; and, now, when our people leave us for other churches, they more often join churches in less hierarchical traditions with more local autonomy.

THE CHANGING NATIONAL CONTEXT

The *Call to Action* also largely ignores the changed national context in which it calls the church to action. I will explain why this is important later; for now, let me rehearse just some of the themes that would inform any serious analysis of the macro-context in which our churches are placed.

- Due to several centuries of secularization, Europe and North America have become "pagan" mission fields once again. Our communities are filled with more and more secular people—who have never been substantially influenced by the Christian faith, who often cannot tell us the name of the church their parents or grandparents stayed away from. Today, the population of the USA exceeds 307 million. At least 180 million of those people are functionally secular. This makes the USA the largest mission field in the western hemisphere and the third largest on earth.
- For more than a century, pre-Christian people were often stuck in the credo of the Enlightment, or the Age of Reason, which produced modernity. In modernity, secular pagans demanded reasons to believe. Today, with the fading of the Enlightenment's influence, postmodern people more likely seek the experiences that would warrant Kierkegaard's "leap of faith."

- The USA has become the most multicultural and multilingual industrialized nation on earth. Approximately 337 languages are spoken in American homes. (Some smaller nations feature more languages. The peoples of Papua New Guinea are known to speak over 840 languages—which makes that island nation an anthropologist's paradise. The average household in Papua New Guinea consists of one husband, one wife, 4.2 children, and one observing anthropologist!) In the USA, 82 percent of our people report English as their mother tongue; that leaves 56 million people who do not. Perhaps half of those people can cope well enough in English to follow a TV program or buy groceries or graduate from high school. But most of them will never be reached through an English-language congregation; the peoples of the nation, and of the earth, are usually reached through their heart language, the language in which they dream.

- A vast number of the secular populations of the USA, English speakers and many others, are more receptive to religious truth-claims and religious options than ever before. Increasingly, lost people in our communities are looking for life, but in all the wrong places. The rise of postmodernity has induced a remarkable new interest, even a hunger, in spirituality. An unprecedented number of people report that they are "spiritual," but not "religious." They try one god after another, from astrology to Zen, in their quest to fulfill their souls. Meanwhile, our churches are strategically placed in the midst of a biblical harvest, but they fail to gather it. People are searching for what the church has to offer, but the church isn't offering it. No mainline denomination is gathering its fair share of the harvest. In a given year, over 40 percent of all United Methodist churches receive no one by profession of faith, not even a child by confirmation. Why? It is the outcome of the widespread mainline approach to evangelism: "Don't ask, don't tell!"

An extended analysis of the harvest would also feature at least the effect of such forces as globalization, urbanization, the media, and changes in the nation's traditional regional cultures and changes in the global popular culture. Many people now live in a TGIF world: Twitter, Google, iPhone, and Facebook. Some churches study the generational cultures; the Builders, Boomers, Busters, and Millennials do seem to have enough differences to take seriously. Some churches do ministry informed by knowledge of the Myers-Briggs personality types; I have observed that INTJ's just do not understand us ESPN's! One church defines its mission fields in terms of the city's zip codes, which may illustrate that some facts are not strategically worth knowing, but some are. If you preach every Sunday, and you are oblivious to the fact that most people today have shorter attention spans than most people a generation ago, then I can tell you one of your problems.

All of this illustrates what organization theorists have long taught us: no organization can effectively understand itself or plan for its future through a closed system analysis that focuses almost exclusively on the organization. If any organization is going to serve and impact its world, open system understanding and planning are required. This book's final chapter will expand on this.

HOW MOVEMENTS ARE DIFFERENT FROM INSTITUTIONS

If we decided that we would not be content to merely revitalize institutional Methodism (if, indeed, that is an option—no mainline denomination has achieved it yet), but would much rather recover something like our earlier experience as a movement, what would that look like? One approach to answering that question would be to learn from the wider study of social movements, especially to discover what all, or most, of the effective social movements have in common. Although not an exhaustive summary of what the study of social movements could teach us, the following top ten insights are indispensable, with obvious implications for the leadership of Christian movements.

1. A movement is an organized network of people with a shared definition of reality, a shared message, and a shared cause with shared objectives. (No would-be social movement that features something like pluralism seems to have enough glue to keep much of anything together.)
2. A movement is not confined to a single campaign. The people are committed for as long as it takes.
3. A movement is distinct from a mere trend in that it is at least minimally organized. Compared to institutions, however, movements are organized more from the bottom up than from the top down, they are more decentralized than centralized, and the movement's local organizations are more autonomous than the United Methodist church down the street. (Leadership of a specific campaign, however, needs to be more centralized and top down.)
4. Within effective movements, multiple organized micro-movements usually flourish. Examples would include the many organizations that share a commitment to peace or the health of creation or the several thousand mission orders within the Roman Catholic Church. We have some micro-movements with United Methodism, such as the Good News movement, the Confessing movement, the Mission Society, and the Council on Evangelism. Serious movements, however, encourage the proliferation of loads of new micro-movements within the movement.
5. Movements usually lack anything like the leverage of bureaucratic power within the organization or the society they hope to change.

They rely on human relations, persuasion, and a consistent message (while refining the message) until the wider organization or society finally "gets it."

6. Effective social movements evangelize all the people they can find who are at all receptive to the cause. The most important factor in whether the movement's cause will ultimately prevail depends on increasing the ranks of serious committed members. (Nominal members and "free riders" are liabilities.) If the movement is perceived as small or declining, it is not taken seriously.

7. Effective social movements continually look for ways to widen their scope and influence and to increase their range of programs and activities, while abandoning programs and activities that are no longer effective.

8. In strong movements, many members root their self-identity, at least partly, in their identification with the movement.

9. Effective movements are fairly flexible. They can change as they learn, as they grow, and as the context changes.

10. Effective movements communicate their vision and message in two steps: (1) They communicate their message publicly, in as many ways as possible. (2) The movement's members then engage people who know about the movement in conversation.

Those ten points from social movement studies have too many implications for Christian movements to spell out here. Fortunately, these insights, when explained, are more understandable than astrophysics; any leader group can study that profile and figure out some things to do to become less institutional and more movemental.

One more lesson from effective social movements merits more elaboration.

HOW EFFECTIVE MOVEMENTS COMMUNICATE

The differences between how movements and institutions communicate to their people and to the public are so stark and so important that communication strategy warrants special consideration. Consider four sets of insights.

First, effective movements communicate their message and mission in distinctive ways: They develop a shared language for talking about the movement's core beliefs and values, but they communicate and interpret these beliefs and values to outsiders in the outsider's language.

Part of the movement's communication agenda is to change people's perception of reality in all three tenses. (1) The movement defines the past for people; this is needed because the part of the past that is relevant to the movement's vision may be unknown, or people may be misinformed. (2) The movement defines the present because many people may perceive no problem that is serious enough to warrant organized action. Often, the movement presents the past and present through a narrative that dramatizes the situation, and often through images, pictures, symbols, music, and theater as well. (3) The movement also communicates a vision of a desirable future than can be attained if the people pull together for long enough, and if they see how they can make a difference.

Second, effective movement leaders keep the vision, and its supporting narrative, ever before the movement's people. They do this by communicating the vision much more often than most people would assume is necessary. (One rule of thumb contends that if you do not reinforce the vision at least monthly, the people tend to forget.) To keep the vision fresh, which mere repetition cannot, movement leaders communicate the vision in as many imaginative ways as possible. And in effective movements, the people have become so immersed in the movement's narrative that they know it by heart, and they can tell it in their own words.

Third, to some degree, an effective movement's leaders are embodiments of the movement's message and purpose. We have known, since Aristotle's *Rhetoric* was published, that the *ethos* of the speaker may be the most influential factor in the communication of a message. Aristotle discovered that if the audience, in a legislature or law court, experiences the speaker as having expertise, character, and good will, the speaker probably has the audience's confidence. For public movement leaders, however, ethos matters enormously more than in legislatures and law courts because movement leaders hope to change people's perceptions of reality, and their identifies, and through them to change the world. In effective movements, the messenger becomes part of the message—as Gandhi was in India, Mandela in South Africa, and King and Chavez in the USA. The movement's leaders must be perceived as credible leaders, who believe in and live for the cause they commend to others. As Lord Soper used to say, "It must mean everything to us before it will mean anything to them."

Fourth, credible movement leaders define their people's identity. Jesus taught his followers that they were "the salt of the earth" (Matthew 5:13) and "the light of the world" (John 8:12). Their identity was contingent upon their connection with him and each other. He was the vine and they were the branches. They were his disciples if they loved one another. If they followed him, he would make them fishers of men and women. The apostles also defined the people's identity. Peter taught his readers, "Once you weren't a people, but now you are God's people" (1 Peter 2:10), and they were "a royal priesthood" (v. 9). Paul informed the church at Corinth that they were "the body of Christ" (1 Corinthians 12:27) and "ambassadors who represent Christ" (2 Corinthians 5:20).

John Wesley seems to have written his "Plain Account of the People Called Methodists," and the "Short History of Methodism," and "The Character of a Methodist" to draw the Methodist people into the grand narrative and the specific theological and ethical vision that defined their identity as "a new people." The same principle seems to be essential in all effective social movements. Cesar Chavez, for example, convinced Hispanic migrant workers of the American Southwest that they were people with dignity who had rights, and if they joined together, they would experience hope and worth.

I first learned about the power of the faith's leaders to define who people are, or can become, from the first generation converts I interviewed. I had assumed (from two degrees in theology) that the gospel was mainly about God and what God did for the world through Jesus Christ and does in us through the Holy Spirit. But when I asked hundreds of converts what, in Christianity's message, especially engaged them, the gospel they heard was as much about themselves as about God. They could usually express the good news they heard about themselves with remarkable cogency, such as "I learned that I am not the junk I thought I was," "The gospel helped me make sense of my life," "I heard the good news that I didn't have to be stuck with the sins that were destroying me and my family," or "If I follow Jesus, my life will be a meaningful adventure." Many converts discovered in Christian teaching and experience a plan or a purpose for their lives.

How do people become open to their leaders telling them who they are? What we know can be cogently stated: If the followers identify with the leaders, and the leaders are credible, and the people know that the leaders understand them and believe in them, the people tend to believe what the leaders tell them about themselves.

OK, it isn't quite that simple. The disclosure needs to be plausible, and it may need to confirm some of their self-perceptions. Furthermore, most people do not usually "get it" the first time. They need to hear who they are—or can be—multiple times over time before they really believe it. There seem to be three stages in the revelation of Christian identity: (1) The gospel reveals who the people are or can become. (2) The gospel calls them to affirm their identity. (3) Decision comes into play; they decide whether or not to accept the call.

Notice two important distinctions: (1) People do not usually decide to believe; faith is a gift, and—like falling in love—many more people, at some point, discover that they believe rather than decide to believe. But people do have to decide to accept their revealed identity, and their new role as a disciple. (2) People do not always discover who they are from the top leaders; many people discover who they are or can be from their peers. This happens especially in small groups, in which people trust each other and are in ministry with each other. Within the experience of koinonia, the people spot strengths and gifts within each other.

In the West, the need for recovering the ministry of identity revelation is more needed now than in a very long time. The 1972 publication of William Glasser's book *The Identity Society* announced a substantial shift in American culture. Until fairly recent history, the USA was a survival society. Most people were driven by the need to put food on the table, pay the bills, provide for retirement, and so on. When those issues seemed to be resolved, at last, many people graduated to an *identity* agenda. Now people, in much greater numbers, ask, "Who am I?" "What am I for?" "What does my life mean?" I meet many people who do not know who they are, or they are profoundly dissatisfied with who they know they have become. To many people, the revelation of their identify, or the new

36

self that they can become, is experienced as great news. Movement leaders tell the people who they are.

CONTAGIOUS CHRISTIANITY

Our final theme is *contagion*. What makes Christianity contagious? We are sufficiently familiar with some of the answers, but four insights are worth repeating. (1) Contagious Christianity is imaginative Christianity. The less prosaic and the more interesting and imaginative the people experience faith's communication, the more contagious it becomes. (2) Ministry that engages people's issues, struggles, and felt needs is more contagious than generic stock presentations of the faith. (3) Enthusiastic Christians contribute to Christianity's contagion. If you do not have enough enthusiastic people in your church, target for outreach some enthusiastic people in the community; they will bring their enthusiasm with them! (4) Growing churches, especially churches receiving converts from the world, are more exciting and contagious than stagnant and declining churches. You can feel the difference when you walk in.

Those four ways we know; but three others warrant some explanation.

CULTURAL RELEVANCE

Culturally relevant expressions of Christianity are much more contagious than culturally alien expressions. The very early Christian movement had to schedule its first "council" to clarify and settle this important strategic principle. Our knowledge of the circumstances and events that led up to the council is sketchy, but it looked something like this:

The very early Christian movement expanded through the proliferation of house churches. Across much of Judea, including Jerusalem, the very early house churches were predominantly Jewish-Christians in their membership. The occasional Gentile converts were welcomed and, like most small minorities, they assimilated to the majority culture. They believed in Jesus as the promised Messiah, they submitted to circumcision, they probably worshiped in Aramaic, and they lived by Jewish laws and customs.

Some Jewish-Christian leaders, including a vocal minority in the Jerusalem church, insisted that Gentile assimilation to the Jewish law and ways was not only desirable in the Judean setting but was *necessary* everywhere. All Gentile peoples, to become Christians, must also become Jews. Scholars doubt that James shared this view; he was the mediating leader between the "Judaizers" and the other local Christians.

When the news came that Gentiles up north in Antioch were becoming disciples and were *not* submitting to circumcision and so on, the Judaizers went ballistic. The Jerusalem church sent Barnabas to sensitize the movement in Antioch, but he fell in love with the movement as it was. The Judaizers were less that satisfied with Barnabas's intervention, so James called a meeting in Jerusalem to settle the matter. At the meeting, Paul advocated a policy that contrasted with the Judaizers' policy by 180 degrees. The faith should *not* impose a single language and culture on the world's peoples; the faith was called to adapt to every tongue and culture on the face of the earth.

With Peter's help, Paul's case prevailed, and the principle of what came to be called "indigenous" Christianity became the policy of the early Christian movement. Acts 16 reports the most important decision ever made to facilitate the expansion of Christianity—in every cultural context, in every age. But it would be an understatement to say that the church has not consistently followed the policy.

For instance, people holding the Jerusalem view did not give up. Judaizers scattered across the Mediterranean world and planted Jewish-Christian churches—while challenging some of the Gentile churches, such as the church at Galatia, to adopt Jewish ways. Again, by some time in the second century, many of the Gentile churches adopted the Jerusalem paradigm in different clothing: the Latin language and Roman customs were now believed to be essential to Christianity's expression and were prerequisite to becoming a Christian, so rural peoples and "barbarian" peoples did not qualify. In time, however, St. Martin reached a rural people and St. Patrick reached a barbarian people by, and not without, recovering the indigenous principle.

Often, the Judaizing principle operates in more informal ways, short of official policy; Christian leaders simply assume that Establishment Christianity's language, customs, and aesthetic are necessary for Christian expression and experience. This was one problem that John Wesley observed in his Church of England in the eighteenth century. The "common people" did not speak establishment Christianity's language. They did not dress, conduct themselves, and enjoy the same kind of music that characterized polite, refined "Christian" society. How could such people become real Christians? You know the rest of the story. Methodism's approach began on the people's turf, and the approach adapted to the common people's style, language, aesthetics, and music, and a contagious movement emerged—of, by, and for the people that establishment Christianity had written off as unsuited for Christianization.

We should not assume, in most of our churches, that we are at all past that problem today. Many secular people are not like "good church people" culturally, and they do not understand stained-glass voices and ecclesiastical jargon. In case you have not noticed, among the unwashed pagan masses, there is no epidemic interest in eighteenth century pipe organ music!

For what it is worth, the policy of cultural relevance has more theological warrant than might be obvious. As Jesus in the Incarnation took on Galilean culture and spoke Galilean folk-Hebrew, so his body, the church, is called to extend such incarnational expressions to every people. Then Paul modeled the way, as he became "all things to all people" that "I could save some by all means possible" (1 Corinthians 9:22). The indigenous principle can be stated in one sentence. Each people's culture is the natural medium for expressing God's revelation to them.

EMOTIONAL RELEVANCE

A second principle behind contagious Christianity is emotional relevance. The European Enlightenment taught that we human beings are unique creatures because we are rational creatures: although we still experience the emotions that we have inherited from our primitive forbears, education has come to lift us into the life of the mind. With the fading of the Enlightenment and the rise of postmodernity, it is becoming apparent that the Enlightenment was wrong by almost 180 degrees. We are not basically rational creatures who sometimes feel; we are basically emotional creatures who sometimes think. Even what we think about is influenced by our background emotional state, and how we think about it is influenced by our feelings at the time.

This discovery is more or less a rediscovery. Even in the eighteenth century, when the Enlightenment's onslaught seemed unstoppable, the romantics found ways to speak to, and awaken, the heart—through poetry, fiction, art, and music. In that same century, Jonathan Edwards reflected upon the indispensable role of "religious affections" in Christian experience, and John Wesley defined Christianity as, substantially, a "religion of the heart."

Today, we need a fuller recovery of a more holistic understanding of human nature, in part because many people in our communities are fighting an emotional war within, and they are being gradually destroyed by emotional forces—like pride, fear, sadness, anger, hate, jealousy, low self-esteem, and other feelings surging within them that are hijacking their lives. Furthermore, authentic Christian conversion involves emotional healing, as well as deliverance from a destructive emotional world into the new emotional world of the kingdom of God, in which such emotions as gratitude, love, humility, peace, healthy self-esteem, and joy enter the convert's experience. The two characters in the film *The Bucket List* edge toward New Testament experiential reality when they agree on life's two most important questions: "Have you found joy in your life?" and "Have you brought joy to others?"

Effective churches begin where people are, including their emotional struggles and their aspirations for emotional freedom. Teaching, counseling, preaching, liturgy, evangelism, and other ministries are expressed with emotional sensitivity and relevance. Indeed, some of us are now suggesting, as Greg Clapper does in his new book, that *The Renewal of the Heart Is the Mission of the Church*. Today, as the recovery ministries of many churches are learning to engage the emotional baggage that attaches to addiction, they are learning to minister to everyone with emotional relevance.

RADICAL OUTREACH

The contagion of culturally relevant Christianity and emotionally relevant Christianity are experienced fairly directly. Take the case of a young man, eight years ago, who is now one of our seminary students. Two Christian friends initiated several conversations with him, and then they invited him to a youth service. As he walked in, good news and hope were being celebrated through music that engaged him; the speaker spoke his language and seemed to understand people like him; and the message offered freedom from the "narcissism" and the "anger issues" that, as he reported, had "tied me up in knots." He found himself responding, and he kept coming back, and he learned all he could; within several months, he was a man of faith. The church's culturally and emotionally relevant ministry engaged him directly.

Another cause of contagion, however, is experienced more indirectly. I have called it *radical outreach*. This point begins very early in the Christian narrative. Jesus and his disciples ministered to people who were blind or deaf or lame, people who were mentally handicapped or possessed, lepers and Samaritans, tax collectors and zealots, and others. You might be surprised to hear that all of those populations, and some others, had one thing in common. The establishment institutional religion of the Temple had written them off. Indeed, the Temple's policy prohibited such people from even entering the temple. Those populations, and others, were officially hopeless. This is the point: Christianity was conceived in the radical outreach that engaged allegedly hopeless people. It typically begins when we visit their turf, and then begin where they are, rather than where we'd like them to be.

As the Christian movement spread to the cities of the Roman Empire, it gradually took a more institutional form, and in time became more like the Temple. Rural populations were not urbane and were, therefore, hopeless. The Goths, the Visigoths, the Franks, the Vandals, the Frisians, the Vikings, and all of the Celtic peoples, including the Irish, were not Latin-speaking, Roman-enculturated people. Obviously, all of those barbarians were not civilized enough to become "Christianized."

This book of tragedy has many chapters, but we do not need to recount the whole volume. Most churches today, in our nation and in our communities, assume that many types of people are unreachable; they assume it would probably be impossible for those people to become real Christians "like us." To be specific, for many churches, pre-literate people, "hard living" people, cohabiting couples, homeless people, bikers, Goths, jet setters, mentally ill people, Mandarin-speakers, people with tattoos, addictive people, introverts, and many others need not apply.

Perceptions, whether they are accurate or not, take on their own reality and when acted upon over time become self-fulfilling prophesies. Take, as one case, the church that had not reached out to any alcoholics within anyone's memory; so understandably, no alcoholics had become Christians in that church in many years. The leaders interpreted this fact to prove that alcoholics were too far gone to become Christians.

But God can use such entrenched assumptions as an occasion for miracles. One woman in that church, a substantial giver with some leverage, sold the board on inviting a local Alcoholics Anonymous group to use a room in the church for their weekly meetings. The woman cultivated several allies in the church, at least two with relatives in recovery, to join her in befriending the facility's new visitors. They prepared hot cocoa and donuts for the Thursday evening meetings, and they provided a nursery for the children. Many of the visitors warmed to the hospitality, and some of them accepted invitations to join their new church friends in Sunday morning worship. In time, several people in recovery joined the church as new Christians. Several of their families started coming, and then more addictive people, and then their families and friends.

The church started a Sunday school class for people in recovery, and then a second class, and support groups for codependent people and for adult children of alcoholics. Several long-time members surfaced, confessing that they had secretly battled addiction for a long time, and they now sought the miracles of sobriety and sanity. In time, miracles became almost commonplace in the church's life. One thirty-something, violence-prone man with a criminal record became obviously transformed; he started helping in the youth ministry. A forty-something woman who once had a "reputation" became an astonishingly caring Christian. Word about the "miracles" spread across the community grapevine. Many people in the community became more responsive. The church grew more than, at one time, it had even wanted to grow!

Using a metaphor borrowed from chemistry, this is catalytic growth. When an athlete takes in Creatine before a workout, the supplement catalyzes an energy source within muscles that permits two or three more bench presses, which in turn catalyzes more muscle growth. In my recent book *The Apostolic Congregation*, I commend the following theory: In every society, apparently, there is an establishment population, and there are fringe populations whom the establishment people regard as impossible or hopeless. Catalytic Christian movements begin when some of the hopeless people are reached, and some of those people experience transparent life change. Such transformations catalyze spiritual openness in many other people, including establishment people, and the faith now spreads, contagiously.

HOW TO GROW YOUR CHURCH

Let me close with an important question: How does a church reach the kinds of decisions that enable it to get its apostolic act together? Sometimes it involves helping leaders get in touch with the assumptions by which they currently navigate the church. Several dozen times, I have asked a United Methodist church's leaders to brainstorm answers to one question: What types of people would *not* be likely to become new Christians in our church? The typical answers include types I have already mentioned and many more. Every leader group has brainstormed twenty types or more; some have thought of thirty types or more. What becomes apparent is that the church mainly wants to reach—or only thinks it can reach—people who are just like the members, only younger. Occasionally, they partly grasp the dilemma: In a denomination that at the general church level most values and demands diversity, most of the denomination's local churches do not value it, or more likely do not assume it is really possible.

What if our assumptions, that so many types of people cannot be reached by our church, are often wrong? What if some contrasting assumptions are often right? What if all sorts of people would respond to saving grace if we believed in them and approached them right?

One church dared to ask such questions: First Baptist Church of Leesburg, Florida—which is now one of the largest churches in one of the smallest cities in the USA. From the early 1980s to the early years of this century, they grew from four hundred members to over seven thousand members.

How did they do that? They reached out to all sorts of people. They discovered that to be helpful and redemptive they could not just invite the people to attend church. *Outreach ministries* were often necessary. To reach addictive people, they started recovery ministries. To reach women who'd once had an abortion, they started support groups. When they reached prisoners in the nearby penitentiary, the warden took a dim view of releasing prisoners every Sunday to go to church, so First Baptist started a satellite congregation in the penitentiary. The church started groups and ministries for ex-prisoners, for divorced people, and deaf people, and for many other people with a range of life conditions. One of First Baptist's large choirs is filled with people in recovery.

This is the nearest thing to a sure-fire approach to church growth there is. With this, no one will finish this book without knowing how to help his or her church grow. If in the future your church does not grow, then that will reflect a choice; you folks decided not to do the one thing that can virtually ensure growth.

What is that one thing? First Baptist Leesburg's growth has essentially streamed from one decision the church's deacons reached in the mid-1980s. Their long-time senior pastor, Charles Roesel, summarizes the decision this way: "We decided to spend our lives befriending and inviting all of the people we could find that no other church seemed to be interested in."

SHAZAM!

Chapter Three

WHY NOT REJOIN THE METHODIST MOVEMENT?

We are asking whether Methodism, in this land, has a long-term future really worth experiencing. I have suggested, with Scott Kisker, that our decision a generation ago to become much less Methodist and much more mainline was a profound and tragic mistake. The first chapter recommended that we move to recover the broad essence of Methodist Christianity, including Wesley's theological vision and the early movement's focus on lay ministry, small groups, and apostolic mission—locally and globally. In chapter 2 I recommended that we become much less like a hierarchical institution and much more like a social movement—with such features as a shared vision, message, and mission; a decentralized organization with much greater local autonomy; and that we take the steps to help our people recover their identity as Methodist Christians. I also recommended that we act to restore Methodism's contagion through culturally relevant ministry, emotionally relevant ministry, and outreach to many types of people beyond the demographic profile of our current membership.

Let's reflect, now, about our future from two theoretical perspectives. Kurt Lewin famously suggested, "There is nothing more practical than a good theory." I am suggesting that two good theories might be twice as practical.

THE APOSTOLIC SUCCESSION THEORY

The first theory has been widely affirmed in most of the major Christian traditions. It is the theory that any expression of Christianity should be in appropriate continuity with the early Christian movement. Most Christian traditions have agreed with that premise most of the time. Pioneers in most Christian traditions have asked what their movement would do, and look like, to be in apostolic succession.

Unfortunately, the Christian traditions have answered the question in too many ways. With some oversimplification, let me illustrate. Roman Catholics have believed that, in ordaining priests, they have a sacramental connection that goes all the way back to the apostles. The Eastern Orthodox tradition believes that their liturgy goes back to the ancient church. Other traditions also use a criterion related to worship; the Adventists, who worship on Saturday, believe that they worship *when* the early Christians worshiped. The House Church movement, now spreading in much of Europe and North America, believes that they worship *where* the early Christians worshiped. The Church of Christ, by not using musical instruments in worship, believes that they thereby worship *how* the early church worshiped. Churches in the Anabaptist tradition often believe that their churches are organized—with local deacons and elders—like the early churches. Churches in the Pentecostal tradition believe that the key is in having the same kinds of spiritual experiences that are reflected in some of the pages of the New Testament.

The Reformers, Luther and Calvin, believed they had rediscovered the theology of the apostles and, therefore, were in apostolic succession. John Wesley also wanted Methodism to be rooted in apostolic Christianity. He believed, with Luther and Calvin, that the theology of the apostles was essential; but Wesley completed the Reformation by adding that Christianity was apostolic if it continued the mission of the apostles and their churches to pre-Christian people. Wesley was not unique in this view. The priority vision to reach pre-Christian populations drove the ancient Celtic Christian movement a thousand years before Wesley, and it drove William Carey, and the birth of the Protestant missionary movement, a generation after Wesley.

Several notable Christian leaders gave this view of missional Christianity fresh expression in the twentieth century. William Temple declared that the true church is "the only society that exists for the benefit of those who are not its members." Emil Brunner declared, "The church exists by mission as a fire exists by burning." C. S. Lewis wrote,

> The Church exists for nothing else but to draw [people] into Christ, to make them little Christs. If [the churches] are not doing that, all the cathedrals, clergy, missions, even the Bible itself, are simply a waste of time. God became man for no other purpose. It is even doubtful, you know, whether the whole universe was created for any other purpose.

THE OPEN SYSTEM THEORY

The second practical theory is rooted in the study of organizations—including churches—and is long identified with three theorists: Schein, Katz, and Kahn. It is called the Open System theory of organizations and features a remarkably simple and visual model.

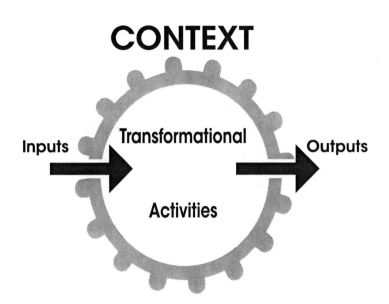

Picture a large circle but with openings on the left and on the right. Everything inside the circle is the organization; everything outside of the circle is the organization's context. According to Open System theory, (a) an organization depends on its context for its very life, and (b) it exists to understand and serve that wider context in ways consistent with the organization's mission; if the organization does not effectively understand and engage the context it is, by definition, irrelevant.

In the Open System model, the opening on the left side of the circle permits inputs to enter into the life of the organization from the wider context. So a church, for instance, would receive from beyond the church the water, the electricity, the building materials, the Bibles, the print and media resources, usually the church's pastor and staff, its theology, and hundreds of other inputs that make the church's life possible. New members are indispensable inputs in the life of a church; every year, a local church has to receive the equivalent of 5 to 7 percent of its present membership just to stay even.

Inside the organization, the leaders engage in throughputs, or transformational activities, to change what has been received from the environment—especially to change the members, new members, and seekers. So the purpose of worship services, Bible studies, prayer meetings, counseling, group life, and a hundred other throughputs is to transform the church's people.

The opening on the circle's right side permits (you guessed it) outputs. By this theory, a church is not an end in itself; it is God's agent in engaging the wider community. As new Christ-followers penetrate the community with the gospel and the Christian social ethic, they work for health, justice, reconciliation, and peace in the community and, in the ministry of witness, they invite the community's people to explore the Christian possibility. Some of those new people are *inputted* into the life of the church, they experience its transformational activities, and they are then sent out as changed people, and so on.

Open System leaders are serious students of their context, and they lead their organizations to adapt to the context in order to serve it. If they do not, they are, by definition, closed system leaders, and their organization's effect upon the context is minimal.

A local church actually functions in regard to two wider contexts—each in widening concentric circles. One of a local church's contexts is its natural context—like the surrounding community, the city, the state, the nation, and the world. A church's immediate natural context includes the community's peoples and the school system and the transportation system and the community's history, government, economy, traditions, and customs. The context also includes factors such as geography and climate. So, for instance, a new church in Southern California could meet in a tent; that strategy would not be available for an Inuit church plant in the Arctic.

A local church's second concentric context is its ecclesial context. A local United Methodist church, for instance, lives within the broader life of a district, a conference, a jurisdiction, and the denomination; other churches and denominations, and world Christianity, are also part of a local church's ecclesial context. Open System theorists would point out that, at each level, the denomination either facilitates or frustrates the local church's local mission. Indeed, the whole system is supposed to exist largely for the sake of the churches and their mission. Ideally, the influence is two-way; local churches may influence the wider church.

THREE PROPOSALS FOR RENEWING CHURCHES

From these two theories, the apostolic succession theory and the Open System theory, and from the perspectives in the first two chapters, we are now in a position to reflect in fresh ways on United Methodism's future. Let's do that in conversation with three public proposals to renew local churches. In the present crisis that institutional Christianity in Europe and in the USA now experiences, there are well over one hundred public proposals for fixing local churches; I am told that there are a dozen such proposals for United Methodism alone. But three proposals for renewing churches are among the best known, and they represent the predominant line of thinking.

Christian Schwarz, a German researcher in the church's service, published *Natural Church Development* in 1996. His research team developed a questionnaire and then surveyed thirty core leaders in one thousand churches, in eighteen languages, in thirty-two countries, over a ten-year period. Reflecting from their data, they staked out a distinctive claim: church growth follows from *church health*; increase a church's health and that brings church growth. So what makes for a healthy church? Schwarz defined *church health* in terms of "eight essential qualities of healthy churches" that his team believed their research identified. Their eight qualities of healthy churches are:

1. Empowering Leadership
2. Gift-oriented Ministry
3. Passionate Spirituality
4. Functional Structures
5. Inspiring Worship
6. Holistic Small Groups
7. Need-oriented Evangelism
8. Loving Relationships

Early in this century, *Natural Church Development* appeared to many church leaders to be the nearest thing to a panacea. Many church leaders in many denominations joined the stampede. Some denominations were not fully satisfied with Schwarz' eight qualities, so they developed their own list. By now, every version of the model seems to have suffered the same fate. Most of these leaders, en masse, have since stepped out of the parade, in part because—in contrast to the Germans' claim—increased health was not reliably resulting in growth.

In 2004, an extensive Presbyterian study resulted in the publication of *Beyond the Ordinary: Ten Strengths of U.S. Congregations*. The coauthors, Cynthia Woolever and Deborah Bruce, identified ten characteristics of strong congregations:

1. Growing Spiritually
2. Meaningful Worship
3. Participation in the Congregation
4. Sense of Belonging
5. Caring for Children and Youth
6. Focusing on the Community (Social Ministry and Advocacy)
7. Sharing Faith with Others
8. Welcoming New People
9. Empowering Lay Leadership
10. Commitment to, and Excitement About, the Congregation's Vision for the Future

Compare the two lists. Many points are identical, or nearly so. The Presbyterians changed *Natural Church Development's* "Inspiring Worship" to "Meaningful Worship." Schwarz's model features laity in ministries; the Presbyterian model does not. The Presbyterians see the need for ministries with children and youth more clearly than the Germans do.

Even more recently, a national United Methodist committee deployed two research teams to gather data from "vital churches." Their *Call to Action*, published in 2010, identifies what they believe to be five drivers of church vitality. Vital churches, they say, have

1. Traditional and contemporary services
2. More small groups than less vital churches
3. More programs for children and youth
4. Pastors who lead planning and preach inspiringly
5. More attendees elevated into leadership roles

The United Methodist *Call to Action* profile of vital churches has much in common with the German and Presbyterian projects. With the Germans, the *Call to Action* knows that small group life contributes to vitality. All three emphasize lay leadership as an important key. The *Call to Action* improves upon *Natural Church Development* at one important point: the German researchers tell us that it makes "no difference" whether a worship service is traditional or contemporary; the Call to Action Committee knows better. Curiously, however, the Presbyterians are clearer than the Germans and the United Methodists that the life of prayer is essential for strong churches. And, in both the German and Presbyterian projects, evangelism is one feature of a healthy, or strong, congregation; but the *Call to Action* assumes the fantasy that a church can increase in vitality without outreach and without inputting new disciples from the community.

What all three proposals have in common, however, is rather remarkable. Let me call your attention to five such features:

(1) All three proposals assume that establishment, institutional, mainline, more or less Eurocentric Christianity is normal Christianity—and many other assumptions flow from that premise. We have seen that a local church's judicatory and denomination are part of its context, and that a local church depends upon the denomination. All three proposals assume, in our vastly changed historical and cultural context, that a denomination's whole inherited system—including its polity and structure, its colleges and seminaries and other institutions, and the pattern for deploying the clergy and governing the denomination—all of that is still the best possible way to organize for the sake of effective local Christianity today. If a local church lacks health or strength or vitality, all three proposals assume that the causes are all local; according to the United Methodist proposal, all the general church needs to do to help

move local churches toward vitality is hold the pastors more accountable. Furthermore, all three proposals assume that nothing is seriously wrong with how we do church, locally; several specific fixes will revitalize our tired old churches.

Keep in mind, these three proposals are but three recent entries in a long line of proposals to renew or revitalize mainline churches. The line of proposals stretches back decades and, so far, no one has succeeded yet in renewing or revitalizing a single mainline denomination. Consider the case of the Presbyterian Church, USA. In 1977, a Presbyterian committee proposed an interesting strategy for arresting their denomination's decline. They would grow again as a result of a two-phase strategy. In the first phase, the Presbyterians would renew their churches across the nation. Then, in phase two, those renewed churches would reach out to unchurched people. That was thirty-four years ago; the Presbyterians have never graduated from phase one!

(2) All three proposals neglect to ask, or even acknowledge, the one question that has been paramount in most of Christian history: How can we do church in continuity with early apostolic Christianity? For almost the first time in church history, the question is now assumed to be not worth asking.

I remember a season in which this shift had become obvious. In the years that I served with the General Board of Discipleship, Ezra Earl Jones became our General Secretary. He discovered that, in the first eight years of its history, the General Board of Discipleship had never defined *discipleship*. So he convened a task force of the Assistant General Secretaries; our assignment was to define the term.

I suggested, in our first meeting, that we begin with a shared understanding of what a disciple was understood to be in the New Testament period. Someone asked, "How would we know that?" I proposed that we all read the article on *mathetes* (disciple) in Kittel's *Theological Dictionary of the New Testament*. Several colleagues resisted and stonewalled the suggestion for several meetings. Finally, we all agreed to "at least read it" before the next meeting. To their credit, they liked it, and the Scriptures partly informed what we finally came up with.

What I encountered in those first meetings, however, was a symptom of United Methodism's (post-1968) early history. Many leaders assumed, and quietly insisted, that the real purpose of the Methodist-EUB merger was to create a new mainline denomination that would be neither Methodist nor EUB; and, in the new denomination, the leaders would get to decide what all of this would now mean. The denominational leaders were "the deciders."

(3) Since 1983, I have taught in the field of Christian mission. The field's biggest consensus recognizes that only "contextualized" expressions of Christianity are likely to be effective in any given field of mission. A contextualization strategy involves studying the host culture and adapting Christianity's expression to the style, the language, the aesthetics, and the indigenous music of the cultural setting in which we hope to plant or expand viable Christianity. Indeed, the great strategic pioneers in Christian mission, from St. Paul and St. Patrick to John Wesley and William Carey, were Open System contextualizing leaders before we knew what to call them.

By comparison, the German, Presbyterian, and United Methodist proposals all reflect more closed-system thinking and planning. For the United Methodist proposal, one example will suffice. The *Call to Action* seems to assume that English language congregations will express the faith for everyone, everywhere. However, since we are called to serve and reach people in the most multi-lingual industrial nation on earth, it makes no more sense to expect to reach almost everyone in English-language congregations than it did for the Roman Catholic Church (prior to Vatican II) to expect to reach and serve everyone in Latin. In other ways, too, most of the *Call's* thinking focuses almost exclusively upon the churches, without serious regard to the changing national context.

All three proposals seem to be oblivious to the changing contextual factors that I featured in chapter 2. Consider the following:

(a) All three proposals ignore the paramount fact that, due to the secularization of the West, Europe and North America have become mission fields once again.

(b) All three proposals ignore the great change of postmodern secular populations more recently: the new quest for spirituality and for meaningful spiritual experience.

(c) In once respect, the *Call to Action* is unique because The United Methodist Church says it wants to transform the world. The problem is that the *Call to Action* does not call local churches to involvement in changing their part of the world. Surely we are not relying on General Conference resolutions to change the world!

In many other ways, the three proposals take the local church's natural context and its ecclesial context less than seriously. The focus is upon local churches, almost exclusively.

(4) None of the three proposals reflects the idea that Christianity is missional Christianity. Although two of the three propose that local

evangelism is one of the eight or ten features of a healthy or strong church, no one suggests that it has anything to do with Christianity's main business; and you would never know from the three proposals that Christianity has a world mission, in which missional Christians live in mission, locally and globally.

(5) A recent conversation with a colleague helped me put the German, Presbyterian, and United Methodist recommendations in better perspective. Each of the three research teams is analogous to a team of medical doctors who write some prescriptions and recommend some surgery—without telling us the diagnosis! The recommended medicine and surgery may be warranted, but an informed patient wants to know why. To be specific, low vitality, in people and in churches, is a symptom. I am told that symptoms in human bodies and in human organizations often have multiple causes. What are the known causes of low vitality in too many of our churches? The *Call to Action* does not tell us.

Let me presume to identify some causes of low vitality. The people called (United) Methodists cannot recall who they are—if, indeed, most of our present members ever knew. They are no longer rooted in the Scriptures or in any recognizable version of Methodism's theological vision; the religion that now inhabits the minds of our attendees is as likely to be Deism or Pantheism or folk wisdom or middle class moralism or civil religion or even astrology or luck, as any recognizable form of "the faith once delivered to the saints."

Continuing the diagnosis: Most of our people who dutifully attend church are like a football team that sits on the bench while supporting, and cheering for, the coach—or they sit on the bench and wish for a better coach! Most of our people are not in ministry within and beyond the church. Most of our churches do not regard Christianity's mission as their main business. Most of our visitors do not experience our churches to speak their language, or engage their emotional struggles; many people in the community, who know they are not like "church people," read signals that we may not really want them. The consequence of all of this, and more, is what John Wesley once feared. What is now called Methodism, in many places, has retained "the form of religion," but "without the power."

Now, that is an attempt at a diagnosis; we could easily add other causes for the malaise that hounds too many of our churches. But those causes, by themselves, could strip congregations of much of the life that many Methodist churches once enjoyed, and I suggest that this is at least part of the diagnosis for which relevant change proposals could make compelling sense.

THE UNITED METHODIST *CALL TO ACTION*

The committee that produced United Methodism's *Call to Action* acknowledges that it is an incomplete plan for renewal. As I studied the document, I became aware of several "great omissions." Let me feature two.

First, you would never know, from the German, Presbyterian, or United Methodist proposals, that church health or strength or vitality has anything to do with theology, or that there could possibly be anything sub-Christian, dysfunctional, heretical, or eccentric about anyone's theology. One of the leaders the father of Australia's Jesus Movement once observed that many churches in the USA are like mules. Naturally, I asked him what he meant. He explained that mules are useful animals, but they are so genetically compromised that they are incapable of reproduction. By this analogy, thousands of our churches are analogous to mules—they are so theologically compromised that they are incapable of reproduction. I have spent time in such churches; they cannot even keep a bare majority of their own children into adult membership. I am not counseling euthanasia for such churches. Like mules, they serve some useful purposes. But don't expect much vitality, much less reproduction; there is not much vitality or reproduction anywhere that the gospel is in absentia.

Second, we have seen that the *Call to Action* is similar to proposals from other mainline leader groups in Europe and North America. So it may be useful to ask: Do such proposals, if implemented, stand a fair change of revitalizing many mainline churches?

Consider a case study. In 1994, Coral Marie Noren moved from the faculty of Duke Divinity School to teach homiletics and liturgics at North Park Seminary in Chicago. That school year, she visited twenty-five mainline churches in Chicago; almost half were United Methodist churches in the Northern Illinois Conference. In each church, she wrote her name and contact information on the registration pad, and in each church she left a contribution by check—with her name and contact information on each check. Out of the twenty-five churches she visited, only five responded to her visit in any way—four with a form letter, one with a phone call; no one visited.

Prepare yourself for a shock: Carol Noren has observed that since 1995 many of those churches have closed! It is understandable; a church has to receive 5 to 7 percent of its membership in new people each year just to stay even. If a church does not even respond to its visitors, it is declining. The reason why United Methodist churches in the Northern Illinois Conference have less than half the membership they had in 1965 is no profound mystery. Without serious interventions, more and more churches, in measurable time, will turn out the lights. Merely involving the remaining members in traditional or contemporary worship and involving more members in small groups and leadership will seldom be enough to reverse the downward spiral.

AMERICAN METHODISM'S MOST DYSFUNCTIONAL SHIFT

I have suggested that Methodism is a special case among the mainline churches (or the *oldline* churches, or the *sideline* churches) of North America. Most of the other mainline denominations came from Europe's established, or nationally privileged, churches that to this day are assumed to be normal Christianity. Methodism crossed the Atlantic, however, as missional Christianity. In England, what the Anglicans saw as a Christian country, the Methodists saw as a mission field. In frontier America, circuit-riding pastors were not appointed to churches; they were appointed to territories. Circuit riders planted churches to reach the people in the communities, and, everywhere, first generation Methodist laity reached far more people than the preachers did. Methodism's outreach was also global; our forbears sent missionaries, in remarkable numbers, to the peoples of many nations. Eight generations of Methodists affirmed, with John Wesley, that the world was their parish.

The *Call to Action* reflects the quiet, but enormous, shift in focus that United Methodism has experienced more recently. The shift can be stated in seven words: We now regard our parishes as our world. We are now concerned that so many of our parishes lack sufficient "vitality."

There may be two problems with the focus on vitality.

(a) Consider the possibility that vitality is a desirable but not sufficient goal for the body of Christ. The quest for mere vitality reflects what is already a diluted and domesticated version of Christianity. A form of Christianity with the power to reach pre-Christian people, rescue the perishing, and change lives and communities has more going for it than a good pastoral leader, more lay leaders, good programs, and two worship styles.

(b) The second problem with the goal of vitality may be that you do not find it by seeking it. You experience life as a by-product of experiencing grace, obeying the will of God, and engaging in ministry and outreach to people; churches, especially, experience greater vitality as a by-product of a stream of once-lost people who are now regularly entering the church's ranks as liberated and changed people. Churches experience vitality as they become involved in the Christian movement far beyond their community—as they support missionaries, as teams of church members join the missionaries in a three-week mission trip to a village in Peru—where they put a roof on a chapel during the day and join in community with the indigenous believers in the evenings. As Bruce Larson observed, "In those three weeks, they do no harm, they do a little good, they discover who they are, and they come back home on fire for mission."

LESSONS FROM WORLD CHRISTIANITY

Meanwhile, across the earth today, movemental churches are rediscovering versions of Methodism's DNA. China serves as a useful case. In 1966, Chairman Mao imposed the Cultural Revolution. He insisted on the total elimination of Christianity and all other foreign influences from China's life. In a decade of persecution, missionaries were deported and pastors were defrocked and churches were closed, but Christianity was not decimated. Instead, the ranks of Christians grew in that decade from four million to thirty million. The growth continues amidst some continuing persecution and tops seventy million today. Brace yourself. There are now, or soon will be, more active Christians in China than in the USA!

How have they done that? See if any of this seems familiar: Christianity in China became largely a lay movement. Chinese Christians reinvented the lay-led house church—in which small to medium-sized groups meet for worship and for ministry with each other. There are now thought to be well over a million house churches in China. Their expression of Christianity is now less foreign; they say it is now "Christianity with a Chinese face." The reports by foreign journalists stress how much they observe a contagious religion of the heart. China's authorities do not permit public events for preaching Christianity. The faith spreads as Christians engage relatives and friends, in the community, in ministry, conversation, and invitation. At the level of basic principles, it is reminiscent of the classical Methodist Way.

The great Christian movements on other continents are mainly lay movements. They find ways to engage pre-Christian populations on secular turf. As the movements mature, they typically discover that holiness really matters. Virtually all of the Global South's very large churches, and many others, are cell-based churches that function as lay movements in the community. They express the faith in culturally indigenous ways and, as Pentecostalism has pioneered, they offer Christianity as an empowering religion of the heart. They engage and reach some of the allegedly hopeless populations in the community, and, as some of those people become miracles, many other people are moved.

Meanwhile, the Church of England has awakened from its long night of slumber. The kind of data that awakened Anglican leaders was finally undeniable. For example, the national British Social Attitudes survey has periodically polled a sampling of the population on a range of questions— including, "Do you belong to any particular religion?" In 1985, 63 percent of the people said they were Christians; in 2010, 42 percent said they were Christians. In 1985, 34 percent said they had "no religion at all"; in 2010, 51 percent (now the majority) said, "no religion at all."

Believe it or not, Anglicans leaders detected a trend in such data! I say that to their credit; many church leaders across Europe and North America are still in denial. Please listen to this: the Anglicans now acknowledge that their whole inherited system, from their ecclesiastical hierarchy to their medieval parish system, is substantially inadequate for the missionary challenge they now face.

So the Anglicans, in cooperation with British Methodism and several other denominations, have launched a "Fresh Expressions" movement. Bishop Graham Cray's book *Mission Shaped Church: Church Planting and Fresh Expressions of Church in a Changing Context* is the movement's major textbook. You can tell by the subtitle that this initiative is rooted in Open System thinking and planning; indeed, the first chapter unpacks the changes in the British cultural context that inform the movement's planning. The most important change in their national context is an enormously bigger change than the declining strength of most of the churches; they now face the death of a national culture that, for a thousand years, socialized the people of England into a kind of "Christian identity."

The Fresh Expressions movement's supreme purpose is to reach pre-Christian people through a missional form of Christianity in every community in the British Isles. The movement is now involving laity on an extravagant scale, in ministries, in leadership, and in starting and leading new local movements. Furthermore, the Anglicans are starting many new churches on the cell group model. Many traditional churches are adding the cell group emphasis and also an alternative missional congregation within their life. (That, by the way, may be the most promising single intervention for renewing a traditional church: 1. You serve the traditional congregation you have inherited; those people will fund the future. 2. You start a more apostolic congregation at the edge; that congregation will enable the church to have a future.)

One day, while attending a seminar led by Bishop Cray on the Fresh Expressions movement, I was reflecting on the movement's major themes—such as small groups, lay ministries, and missional congregations in every community. Hmmm. It all sounded strangely familiar! When I asked Graham Cray if, perhaps, this Anglican movement's very existence is an admission that John Wesley was right after all, he smiled. A big smile!

Worldwide, the validity of the basic principles of Methodism has never been more universally demonstrated and dramatized than they are today. I'd like to propose an idea: Why don't we join the parade? We have forfeited our opportunity to lead the parade, but we could join it! With all of our shifting to the mainline paradigm, are there any reasons to believe that we have in fact improved on Christianity according to the Wesleys? Why not recover—and run with—a version of classical Methodism that is appropriate for our time and context? Do we have anything better to do?

John and Charles Wesley and the early Methodists often reminded each other of the Methodist movement's main business. In 1744, in a letter to John, Charles Wesley reflected Methodism's apostolic vision in these lines:

> When first we set forth to minister the Word,
> Say, did we preach ourselves, or Christ the Lord?
> Was it our goal disciples to collect,   .

To raise a party, or to found a sect?
No. But to spread the power of Jesus' name,
To repair the walls of our Jerusalem,
To revive the faith of ancient days,
And to fill the earth with our redeemer's praise.

CPSIA information can be obtained at www.ICGtesting.com
Printed in the USA
LVOW011601291211

261577LV00001B/1/P